Dedication

This book is dedicated to the International Association of Travelers (IAMAT). Founded more than 30 years ago, this organization provides valuable, free information on disease risk, climate, sanitation conditions and a list of doctors who can help you if you become ill or hurt on a trip. Membership is free. IAMAT is financed entirely by voluntary donations. To join contact IAMAT at 417 Center Street, Lewiston,NY 14092, telephone (716) 754-4883 or 40 Regal Road, Guelph, Ontario, N1K 1B5, telephone (519) 836-0102.

David R. Scott
Valparaiso, IN

William W. Forgey, M.D.
Crown Point, IN

Foreword

Few things in life are more rewarding or more educational than travel. Although at times costly, travel provides one with a greater sense of culture, geography and accomplishment. But beyond all that, and most important, travel offers the best gift of all…travel offers the gift of memories.

A good friend of mine once said,"Better to buy experiences, rather than things."

Things collect dust, *memories* on the other hand collect emotion and wisdom. Now, sometimes these memories are humorous, sometimes touching and sometimes down-right terrifying. None-the-less, they are irreplaceable and the more one travels the more memories he or she collects. Regardless whether or not these memories are good or bad, there is always something to be learned hidden within each.

Having spent various periods of time in unique places around the globe and associating with people who have done likewise, Doctor Forgey and I have compiled a well-spring of tips, tricks and shortcuts that may help you or someone you know have a more pleasurable traveling experience.

This book includes everything from pre-trip planning to currency exchange; from general health and safety, to passport savvy. You've already got the guts…and now you've got the gear. So what are you waiting for? The world is a mighty big place and life is too short not to see at least some of it. So go on, pack up and move out, and just to make your life a little easier pack this book in one of your bags. You can thank us for it later.

TRAVELER'S LITTLE BOOK OF WISDOM

A Couple Hundred Suggestions, Observations
and Reminders for Travelers to Read,
Remember and Share.

By David Scott & William W. Forgey M.D.

ICS BOOKS, Inc.
Merrillville, IN

Traveler's Little Book of Wisdom

Copyright © 1996 by David Scott & William W. Forgey M.D.

10 9 8 7 6 5 4 3 2 1

All rights reserved, including the right to reproduce this book or portions thereof
in any form or by any means, electronic or mechanical, including photocopying,
recording, unless authorization is obtained, in writing, from the publisher.

All inquiries should be addressed to ICS Books, Inc, 1370 E. 86th Place, Merrillville, IN 46410

Published by:	**Co-Published in Canada by:**	**Printed in the U.S.A.**
ICS BOOKS, Inc	Vanwell Publishing LTD	All ICS titles are printed on 50% recycled paper fro
1370 E. 86th Place	1 Northrup Crescent	pre-consumer waste. All sheets are processed witho
Merrillville, IN 46410	St. Catharines, Ontario	using acid.
800-541-7323	L2M 6P5	
	800-661-6136	

Library of Congress Cataloging-in-Publication Data

Due to government shutdown, no CIP information was available at press time.
Please call ICS BOOKS and we will be glad to fax CIP information when available.
Call toll free 800-541-7323

1.   If you secure your passport in a hotel
      safe, don't forget it on departure.

2.   If in doubt about the safety of the water,
      also avoid the use of ice—freezing does
      not kill germs.

3.   Find out what shots you may need two months before traveling abroad.

4. Never let a mere acquaintance watch your bags.

5. Never leave your luggage unattended, it will be picked up by airport security.

6. Collect frequent flyer miles with any airline you happen to fly.

7. Remember that the laws for driving in a foreign country are not as they are here. Use caution.

8. Don't shout if someone cannot understand you.

9. Constantly be aware of the time changes, reset your watch as you travel.

10. Constantly be aware of the currency exchange, check the Wall Street Journal for current rates.

11. Always be discreet with your money.

12. Attempt to pack light; you'll be glad you did.

13. Try to pack slightly less than your luggage can carry. This way you will have room for souvenirs.

14. Don't forget to bring any prescribed medications.

15. Check with the appropriate embassy to make certain you will have no problems getting that medication into specific countries.

16. Carry these and other medications on board the plane with you in case your checked baggage gets lost.

17. Always respect the customs of other countries.

18. Read about your destination before going there . . . not while you're there.

19. Be aware, and never underestimate a pick-pocket's talents.

20. Understand the country's sizing charts before purchasing clothing.

21. Never spray-paint cars in Singapore…does the name Michael Fay mean anything to you?

22.   Store backpacks in large plastic bags before checking them in. This will save the straps.

23.   Always allow plenty of check-in time before your plane departs, especially during times of increased security.

24. Airlines request you be there at least two hours prior to international departures.

25. Understand and abide by all laws.

26. Bring some anti-diarrhea medication such as Imodium A-D®.

27. Remember, in some countries public displays of affection are taboo.

28. Always know which items must be declared at customs.

29. Don't expect special treatment just because you're a foreigner.

30. Use caution when displaying hand signals. For example, in the Middle East, the thumbs up sign is an obscene gesture.

31. Trust your instincts.

32. Women . . . don't leave purses laying on the floor while in the stall of a bath room.

33. Have your travel documents ready for the customs official, but don't include unnecessary papers with them.

34. Attempt to refrain from drinking too
     much alcohol on long flights.

35. Do, however, drink plenty of water.

36. If hand signals cannot penetrate the language barrier, draw a picture.

37. Different countries often times have different electrical currents. You might consider purchasing a current converter. (Usually no more than $20.00 U.S.)

38. Avoid picking up hitch-hikers.

39.   If you spend over $400.00 (U.S.), you may be charged duty tax.

40.   Wrap presents so they can be easily undone by customs officials.

41. Use caution when letting a stranger take your picture.

42. Use caution when taking pictures of strangers, especially guards, religious people or government officials.

43.　　Take along plenty of film.

44.　　Film from your vacation should be
considered a valuable commodity.
Carry it on the plane instead of
checking it.

45. Store film in lead envelopes; ask for them at your local camera shop.

46. Don't forget that film in checked bags may be X-rayed as well.

47. Try to get yourself in some of the pictures.

48.   Vary your picture taking.

49.   Buy some "Hard-Rock-Cafe" T-shirts.

50.   Give one to a friend back home.

51. Drug trafficking in some countries is punishable either by death, or several years in a prison where only half of the inmates survive.

52. Parole is a foreign word in most foreign prisons.

53. Have someone pick up your mail while you're away.

54.   Store money in a money belt.

55.   Carry a telephone calling card.

56.   Use caution when bartering at street-side markets; the "name-brands" are most often imitations.

57.　Make certain the clothing you bring matches the climate you will be in. Contact IAMAT see number 354.

58.　Never underestimate the weather.

59.　Turn off all home appliances before leaving.

60. Lock all doors, windows, and valuables securely before leaving.

61. Substitute as much glass as you can with plastic containers.

62. Tape your name, address, and phone number inside your luggage. Sometimes your name tags get ripped off the luggage.

63. Do not bring food home as gifts.

64. Many countries have a significant bureaucracy, but few are as advanced or aggravating as the U.S.

65. Remember, some countries are not developing, they are retrogressing.

66. Be aware of those around you.

67. Carry with you the name, address, and phone number of your hotel.

68. Know how to say your hotel name in the native tongue.

69. Allow time for your body to adjust after a long flight. It usually takes at least two days.

70. Always try to walk around with a friend as opposed to alone.

71.   Keep your children close at all times.

72.   Explain to your children where to go if they become lost.

73.   Make sure your children know the name of your hotel.

74.   If you must separate, have a
       designated meeting time at an
       obvious place.

75. Store containers with liquids inside plastic bags.

76. Always bring extra plastic bags.

77. Chances are, if the price of a trip sounds too good to be true, it probably is.

78. Know what parts of town to avoid.

79. Pack a pocket flashlight.

80. Since most temperature ratings are in Celsius, multiply the "C" rating by 2, and add 30 for an approximate Fahrenheit temp. For an accurate rating, multiply by 1.2, and add 32.

81. Carry a map and a phrase book.

82. If traveling in a cold climate, rely on a layering system of clothing.

83. When traveling in a hotter climate, rely on loose fitting cotton clothing.

84. Rain gear should almost always be on your list of items to bring.

85. If you think you may be doing a lot of walking, consider hiking boots as opposed to athletic shoes.

86. Don't forget to bring a small sewing repair kit.

87. Leave the phone number of your hotel with someone at home in case of an emergency.

88. Make sure your bills are paid in advance before you leave.

89. Always bring along a pair of sunglasses.

90.   If your ears pop during a flight, chew bubble gum or blow your nose.

91.   Make the time to learn, see, and experience the culture of the country you are visiting.

92.   Pack a good hat that matches the environment you will be in.

93.   If you don't believe you will use it…don't bring it along.

94. When traveling in third world countries, carry some sort of water purification.

95.   Bring a small day or fanny pack to carry loose items when walking abroad.

96.   If you go on a guided tour, bring your own bottled water.

97.   Ask your travel agent about any special "vacation package deals" your airline might have.

98.   Travel a lot? Consider purchasing a home travel agent for your computer. These days you can reserve a plane ticket, hotel room, rental car, and check for the best fares, all from the confines of your home.

99.   When deciding on a vacation spot, don't neglect different parts of the U.S.

100. Bring a few small travel games when traveling with children.

101. Save all of your receipts.

102. Never leave valuables in your luggage, always carry them on board the plane.

103. Bring along some snacks for the trip.

104. Make sure all snacks are in sealed packages if you must take them through customs.

105. If allowing your bags to be checked by a porter, always leave a good tip.

106. Be cautious when letting a porter check your bags in a foreign country.

107. Don't forget that a Swiss Army knife is one of the world's great travel tools.

108. Do not pack that knife in your carry-on luggage while flying.

109. Motion sickness tablets…need I say more.

110. Consider taking a video camera.

111. Don't forget its battery charger.

112. Make an effort to pack with some sense of organization.

113. Forget attempting not to look like a tourist.

114. Use your time wisely. Don't fly to some exotic spot on the globe only to sit in your hotel room and watch melodramatic foreign soap-operas.

115. With an American Express, Visa, Master Card, or Diners Club, you can obtain cash in just about every major city in the world.

116. Try to remember your pin number.

117. If you cannot remember the number, write a scrambled version of the PIN on the card.

118. Photocopy all of your travel documents.

119. Don't pack those copies in the same bag as your originals.

120. Before asking for a fork, try the chop sticks.

121. Don't forget to pack any personal hygiene items you may need.

122. Ask the locals where to find the best food, sights, and bargains.

123. Bring plenty of reading material for the flight.

124. Or, bring a laptop computer. Long flights are great places to get work done.

125. Make certain you don't have to pay first before using a restroom.

126. In some countries, the toilet is a hole in the ground and the toilet paper is a bucket of water. (Now you know why many people in different countries don't eat, shake hands, or wave with the left hand.)

127. Pack a small travel iron.

128. Always remember that you are a representative of your country.

129. Purchase a watch that displays more than one time zone.

130. Make sure that watch also comes with an alarm.

131. Learn how to ask a few basic questions
      in the native tongue.

132. Try shopping in some of the airports'
      duty-free shops.

133. Go on an organized city tour.

134. Don't be surprised to hear the tour guide repeat himself in as many as four different languages.

135. If your tour guide does a good job, tip him/her appropriately.

136. Always confirm the rate with a cab driver before getting into the cab.

137. Make sure that the taxi you climb into is well marked and appears to be legitimate.

138. Always wear your seat belt in a taxi, here in the states or abroad.

139. Bring with you one nice set of dress clothes.

140. Don't forget the accessories that go with those nice clothes, i.e. dress shoes, socks, belt, tie, etc.

141.   Whenever possible, use carry-on luggage to avoid checking bags.

142.   Ask an employee of your airline how many carry-on bags you're allowed.

143.   The maximum "under-seat" carry on luggage size is: 20x15x10.

144. Buy some souvenirs.

145. Before buying a watch in a foreign country, make sure you can buy batteries for it in the states.

146. Never try to bet against a street-side con artist. The odds are more than stacked against you.

147. Work out some sort of spending plan before your departure so you don't end up broke when you get home.

148. Try walking from sight to sight in order to see how the locals live.

149. Purchase some hand-made clothing or crafts.

150. Most airlines can arrange to serve you special meals i.e. vegetarian, diabetic, or children's meals. Ask your travel agent well in advance.

151. Be wary of unaccompanied dogs on the street even if they do look friendly.

152. If you have problems with long flights, ask your doctor for safe, mild sleeping aids.

153. Be aware that many airports have restricted parking and unloading zones due to security regulations.

154. Always wear your wallet deep in your front pockets, (especially in China and Italy where they are known for pick-pocketing.)

155. Don't forget to exchange your money before returning home.

156. Some countries will not let you take their currency across their borders.

157. Coffee in some countries may be three or four times stronger than coffee you are used to in the states.

158. Know where the nearest U.S. Embassy is located.

159. Have your travel agent provide you information about trip insurance and medical treatment and evacuation insurance.

160. Make certain you know what you're eating if you can't understand the menu. Sheep eye-balls and chilled monkey brains are a delicacy in some parts of the world.

161. Sometimes, however, it is better not to ask what you are eating as long as it is adequately cooked.

162. Bring along some antacid in case some of those foods don't agree with your system.

163. Frequent flyer miles are a wonderful way to travel for free. Don't forget that many hotels and rental car agencies award F.F. miles as well.

164. If you happen to get diarrhea, drink juices with a pinch of salt to replace lost potassium and sodium.

165. Even though it may cost a little more, try to stay in a safe hotel.

166. Make certain your luggage is easily identifiable and won't be mistakenly picked up by someone else.

167. Don't complain about rough baggage handling, it's always been that way. Just buy a better suitcase.

168. Send home plenty of postcards.

169. Don't "rub-in" the fact that they are not enjoying a great trip like yours.

170. Before you buy that three-gallon egg-shell china serving bowl, consider how you will get it back home in one piece.

171. Make an effort to keep your hands free when walking about.

172. When absent, make your room seem occupied; leave the T.V. on.

173. When asked what the purpose of your trip is, always reply "pleasure," unless you are traveling on a business or special visa.

174. Always insure packages being sent home.

175. Don't leave unprotected valuables in your room.

176. Have a neighbor park in your driveway while you're gone.

177. Bring along your own supply of toilet paper.

178. Call the airport in advance to make sure your flight is on time.

179. Don't forget your bags in the overhead compartment.

180. Also, check the seat pocket in front of you or avoid using it for storing very valuable items or documents.

181.   Determine whether or not you are
       physically capable of handling your
       journey.

182.   If you can't decide, ask your doctor
       what he thinks.

183. Don't be overly paranoid.

184. Don't be too secure either.

185. Know your blood type.

186. Carry a medical summary card if you have medical problems.

187. Know if you must obtain a visa before you leave on your trip.

188. Allow plenty of time for applying for a visa.

189. Do not pack your passport in your check-in luggage.

190. Check all your receipts to make certain the numbers have not been altered.

191. Avoid renting a car and attempting to drive in the Orient.

192.   Familiarize yourself with the area
       where you are staying.

193.   Memorize your passport number.

194.   Water, in some countries, is not always
       free.

195. See the country from the window of a train or boat, as opposed to a plane.

196. Be wary of air-war deals. Getting a seat is not always as easy as it seems.

197. Avoid crossing your legs on long flights. This impedes the circulation and promotes blood clots.

198. If using a blanket while sleeping on a plane, fasten your seat belt over the blanket in order not to be disturbed.

199. When doing business overseas, bring plenty of business cards, and have one side printed in the local language.

200. Don't use 800 numbers on foreign business cards, use the area code and direct dial number instead (unless you have an international 800 number.)

201. Know how to access the country's telephone emergency care number.

202. Remember to use the security lock on your hotel room door.

203. Use a credit card that has a medical assistance plan.

204. Pack a pair of fine pointed tweezers, they always come in handy.

205. While checking into a hotel, ask if your room has smoke alarms.

206. Make sure you know how to turn the damn thing off if it starts to ring because of steam from the shower or something of that nature.

207. Don't stay above the seventh floor for easier fire rescue.

208. The best form of communication, world wide, is a smile.

209. If you want to learn about a specific country, go there. Travel is the best education you can get.

210. Choose a travel partner wisely, making sure you'll be able to get along, and work together.

211. Always read the fine print.

212. When traveling with a friend, schedule some time apart.

213. Start making plans far in advance. Ask yourself as well as your travel companions what it is you all wish to do and work from there.

214. A positive attitude is the most important element in successful travel.

215. Hunt around for a good travel agent.

216. Make sure they understand that you demand the best deal available.

217. Avoid making international phone calls from your hotel room, the fee may be triple what you normally pay.

218. U.S. passports are valid for ten years, but only 5 years when obtained under the age of 18.

219. The cost of a new passport is $35.00 plus a $7.00 processing fee.

220. You may apply for a passport by mail. Check with your local government office, i.e. courthouse or post office.

221. To apply for a passport you need: two recent, identical photos (2 inch square) of yourself (available at most photo shops), a copy of your birth certificate bearing its issuing seal, and one other form of identification such as a driver's license.

222. If you have changed your name include with your renewal application a copy of your marriage license or certified court order verifying your name change.

223. Avoid delays by applying for your passport in person at a passport agency.

224. Boston, Chicago, Honolulu, Houston, L.A., Miami, New Orleans, New York, Philadelphia, San Francisco, Seattle, Stamford and Washington D.C. are the thirteen passport agencies located in the U.S.

225. Always pack your common sense, especially when traveling solo.

226. Avoid purchasing food (unless hot and freshly cooked) or liquor from street vendors.

227. If driving in a foreign country, first become familiar with the international road signs.

228. Get plenty of sleep the night before flying.

229. Write out your itinerary including addresses and phone numbers and leave it with someone you know at home.

230. If you are a member of a frequent flyer club, save all of your ticket receipts in case you are not credited for your miles.

231. Make sure your luggage will be checked through to your final destination.

232. If you travel a lot, buy a suitcase with locks.

233. Never throw away your luggage claim checks until you have left the airport.

234. Always remove any old destination tags from your luggage.

235. On long flights, walk around the cabin of the plane every hour or so to help with your blood's circulation.

236. If you haven't memorized it by now, pay attention to, and understand all flight safety instructions before taking off, especially the nearest exit in either direction from your seat.

237. If possible, wear comfortable, loose-fitting clothing while flying.

238. Pack a toilet kit in your carry on bag so you can shave etc. before landing.

239. Afraid of flying? Bring a good book.

240. If there is a row of empty seats on the plane, ask the flight attendant if you may move in order to stretch out.

241. Because of the cabin's dry air, keep yourself hydrated.

242. Avoid eating too much on long flights.

243. In the unlikely event of a hijacking, ask and see if you will receive frequent flyer miles for the re-routed trip.

244. Try not to plan several events after a long flight.

245. When checking in, make sure the ticket agent tags each bag.

246. Leave sex on the beach at the bar; it's a drink not an activity.

247. When children are near water, watch them constantly.

248. Freezing water does not kill the germs within; avoid ice.

249. In accordance with the above, drink hard liquor straight up; better to stir the brain than the bowels.

250. Always practice good hygiene at home and abroad.

251. When trekking and eating from roadside vendors, have them place hot food directly into your personal plastic bowel and cup. Many germs come from their washing dishes along the road side.

252. As opposed to drinking straight from the bottle, bring your own cup.

253. When in Rome…well, you know the rest.

254. Ask for a comment card to commend or condemn your airline's performance.

255. Fear can hold you prisoner...dreams can set you free.

256. Try just once in your life to fly international first-class, it is a journey you will never forget. Use those frequent flyer miles to upgrade.

257. A journey of a thousand leagues begins with where the feet stand.—Lao Tzu

258. A good traveler leaves no tracks.
—Lao Tzu

259. Take chances, not risks.

260. Don't steal hotel towels unless you don't mind paying the fee.

261. Carry a dummy wallet with a small amount of cash in it that you can give to a thief if accosted.

262. Get to your luggage on the carousel before someone else does.

263. Fly a lot? Join an airline club i.e. The Red Carpet Club or The Admirals Club, etc.

264. Buy cosmetics in the sample section of your drugstore. They come in perfect travel sizes.

265. Never buy melons by weight, only by size. Some street vendors inject the melons with water.

266. Don't trust local brands of bottled water.

267. Examine brand name water for counterfeit.

268. Carbonated water is less apt to be counterfeit.

269. All of your constitutional rights are lost when you leave the U.S.

270. If something is wrong at the check-in counter, be kind and courteous.

271. If that doesn't work, be pathetic.

272. If that doesn't work, be irate.

273. Questioning restaurant sanitation? Check out the bathrooms.

274. Never swim where locals won't.

275. If teenagers are the only ones swimming, don't. They take too many chances in unsafe conditions.

276. Know what's in the water before jumping in.

277. Avoid swimming or walking on the beach barefoot.

278. Villages and resorts in third world countries often dump raw sewage directly into the ocean or nearest body of water.

279. If they don't know what a "restroom" is ask for a "watercloset."

280. Avoid saying at all costs, "I'll figure it out when I get there."

281. Home is where the heart is.

282. When deciding on things to do, schedule some relaxation time.

283.   Don't forget, that in some countries showing the bottom of your foot can be a tremendous insult.

284.   Keep a daily schedule.

285.   Don't let it keep you.

286. Buy large souvenirs at the end of your trip.

287. Beware of local social customs when giving gifts.

288. Don't ship gifts overseas without first knowing what the tax will be.

289. Make the value of a gift equal to the services rendered or friendship felt.

290. Make house gifts appropriate to the decor.

291. It's equally inappropriate to overspend as it is to underspend.

292. Sometimes the best gift is a sincere letter of thanks.

293. When bringing gifts from the U.S., bring gifts that are lightweight, have high tax values, and are typically American, i.e. duty-free amounts of American liquor, tobacco, and cosmetics.

294. Do not call an Austrian a German, or an Australian.

295. Try to leave the expensive jewelry at home.

296. If your hotel room has a bar, avoid using it, the prices are stiff.

297. Keep your appearance commendable. Just because you're on vacation doesn't mean you can look like a slob.

298. It's more important what you do than where you go from a disease standpoint.

299. When leaving your hotel room, make sure the door is completely shut and locked.

300. If you feel it appropriate, use the hotel's safe deposit box.

301. Don't leave your hotel key in the open when taking advantage of the hotel's swimming pool or bar.

302. If you don't ask for a discount, you won't get one.

303. Avoid sleeping in until noon. Get up and see how the day begins, no matter where you are.

304. If you're traveling on a train that makes stops in other countries, you may need a visa for those countries even if you don't leave the train.

305. Traveler's checks often receive a better exchange rate.

306. You will need your passport to cash traveler's checks.

307. Bring half the clothes and twice the cash.

308. Remove your shoes and try to elevate your feet during long flights.

309. Bring a Walkman™ on board the plane to listen to your favorite music.

310. If you are giving a business slide presentation, carry those slides on the plane with you.

311. Try the wakeup call…but don't depend on it.

312. When standing with your suitcase behind you, always tilt it so that it rests against your leg. You will be aware if someone suddenly grabs it.

313. Count your bags each time you get off the plane, train, or taxi.

314. Do not leave loose straps hanging from your luggage. They may be easily torn off.

315. Always watch the customs official if he goes through your bags.

316. In some countries, especially heavy tourist areas such as Jamaica, local people will demand money for pictures.

317. Always try to keep your sense of adventure.

318. While traveling by train, make sure you sit in the correct car, otherwise your car might go to a separate destination.

319. On a train in Europe, a sleeper is a bedroom, and a couchette is an open bunk, with no privacy.

320. Remember that taking an earlier connecting flight may cause your bags to travel at a different time. This may be illegal in some foreign travel, and bags that arrive without you may be secured in many domestic airports.

321. Always examine your hotel bill carefully.

322. Ask when checking into a hotel about express checkout. This will save you a great deal of time later.

323. When renting a car, check for dents or other damage and insist these findings be noted in writing by the rental agent.

324. Pay attention to the airport monitors for any flight delays.

325. Bring along a roll of duct tape. With it you can repair almost anything.

326. Also, when traveling with small children, pack a roll of paper toweling.

327.   Try to stay regular. Even if you don't have to go, consider possible future inconvenience when passing up a toilet facility.

328.   Avoid letting your children eat ice cream or other dairy products in third world countries.

329.   Ditto for yourself.

330. If you don't mind the wait, let someone else on board a full plane and take a later one. You will usually be awarded a free ticket or flight credits for doing so.

331. If you don't know the name of your hotel in the native tongue, mark it on a map so the cab driver knows where to go.

332. Keep a mental note of where the nearest fire exit is, either on the plane or in your hotel room.

333. When attempting to speak a foreign language, do not be discouraged by failure, just keep trying.

334. Sitting toward the front of the aircraft will provide a smoother, quieter ride. But most people survive plane crashes when sitting near the tail of the plane.

335. Ask for an exit aisle when you check in. The seats in front do not recline as much so you have more room.

336. Keep a scrap book that details each one of your trips.

337. Bring along a pocket calculator to help you figure out the exchange rate.

338. When buying a suitcase, buy one with a set of sturdy wheels if you foresee carrying heavy loads or walking great distances.

339. Three most important elements in travel (in order of importance): companions, gear, destination.

340. Eat well to sleep warm.

341. Look at but don't touch relics in places of historical significance.

342. Always share your goodies, be it with
      your travel companions or the locals.

343. When trekking in South America and
      Central America, avoid Chagas'
      Disease by using netting over beds and
      sleeping bags.

344. Travel irons are prohibited on most cruise ships because of their potential fire hazard; check with your travel agent.

345. If pregnant, ask your doctor before taking any motion sickness tablets.

346. Dave's mother swears by a product called "Quezzy-Aids." A pair of small devices that are worn on the wrists to prevent motion sickness.

347. Some rental car agencies will not rent cars to people under 25 or over 70.

348. Carry more traveler's checks than cash.

349. Store unused film in the refrigerator to avoid deterioration.

350. Bring a notarized copy of your birth certificate as well as extra passport photos.

351. Bring sunblock whether you will be in sun or in snow.

352. Write your ticket numbers down in case you misplace the actual ticket itself.

353. It's better to be home wishing you were traveling, than traveling wishing you were at home.

354.   Join IAMAT. It's free (they do appreciate donations) and they have a list of doctors that can treat you around the world and extensive information on travel hazards, immunizations, etc. (417 Center St. Lewiston, NY 14092) Telephone (716) 754-4883.

355. Make sure your tetanus immunization is up to date, even if you do not plan to travel.

356. If traveling to any developing nation, obtain hepatitis A and typhoid immunizations.

357. Certain countries require yellow fever vaccination. This shot can only be obtained from specific centers. Check with your county board of health for locations.

358. There is nothing like staying home for real comfort.

– Jane Austin

359. "When asked if I had been uncomfortable on the trip, I didn't really remember. The next time I paid attention and found that, indeed, I was frequently uncomfortable, but that it really didn't matter, for the discomfort only heightened the senses and the value of the trip."

– Doc Forgey

360. Always carry a picture ID.

361. Boiling water will kill any germs that will cause diarrhea.

362. Meningitis immunization should be obtained when visiting parts of Africa, Nepal, and India.

363. Until a new serum is developed, the cholera vaccine is not worth taking.

364. When visiting central Africa, adults should have a one-time booster of the polio vaccine.

365. Treat clothing with .5% permethrin to keep ticks, fleas, chiggers and other bugs from biting.

366. When using deet insect repellent, avoid concentrations of greater than 35% on your skin.

367. When traveling in rural areas of Southeast Asia for 3 weeks or longer, consider obtaining a Japanese Encephalitis vaccine.

368. Start obtaining immunizations at least 8 weeks prior to leaving.

369. When airport officials ask about your luggage, assure them that you packed it and kept it under surveillance at all times.

370. Swimming in fresh water streams and lakes in tropical areas? Be aware of safari fever or schistosomiasis.

371.   Smallpox has been wiped off the face of the earth and no longer exists except in a Russian and U.S. laboratory.

372.   The incidence of polio is decreasing and it no longer exists in the New World.

373.   The incidence of cholera is increasing and is in most developing nations of the world.

374. When aggravated by long lines at customs in foreign countries, note what non-U.S. citizens have to go through when entering our country.

375. The U.S. Embassy cannot recommend an attorney to you overseas, but they can give the list prepared for them by the local Bar Association.

376. The U.S. Embassy cannot provide you with medical help overseas, but sometimes the Russian or various allied embassies will.

377. In undeveloped countries, be prepared to pay for medical care with cash.

378. When all else fails, seek medical help at a university hospital.

379. Keep a list of medicines taken overseas and show them to your doctor when you return home.

380. If you become ill while traveling, have a physical when you return home, even though you feel well.

381. Even years later, always remember that your travel history is now part of your medical history.

382. Lost passports can be replaced at the American Embassy.

383. Receiving a replacement is <u>not</u> an overnight deal.

384. You cannot leave most foreign countries without one.

...s of Wisdom Series

910.202
Scott, David
Traveler's little book
of wisdom
[34077259] (1996)

xims, precepts,
& epigrams

• 365 ma...

• 160 pages

6 x 4 1/2

.95 ($7.95 Canada)

Parent's Little Book of Wisdom by Tilton / Gray ISBN 1-57034-039-0
Writer's Little Book of Wisdom by John Long ISBN 1-57034-037-4
Bachelor's Little Book of Wisdom by David Scott ISBN 1-57034-038-2
Traveler's Little Book of Wisdom by Forgey, M.D. / Scott ISBN 1-57034-036-6
Canoeist's Little Book of Wisdom by Cliff Jacobson ISBN 1-57034-040-4
Teacher's Little Book of Wisdom by Bob Algozzine ISBN 1-57034-017-X
Doctor's Little Book of Wisdom by William W. Forgey M.D. ISBN 1-57034-016-1
Camping's Little Book of Wisdom by David Scott ISBN 0-934802-96-3

For a FREE catalog of all ICS BOOKS titles Call 1-800-541-7323
e-Mail us at **booksics@aol.com** or look for us at **http://www.onlinesports.com/ics**

BACHELOR'S
LITTLE BOOK
of
Wisdom